STRIVING *for the* BOTTOM

Discover Your True Identity
Embrace Your Purpose and
Develop the Power to Elevate Others

CHAD OWEN

emerge
publishing

TULSA, OKLAHOMA

24 23 22 21 20 19   8 7 6 5 4 3 2 1

STRIVING FOR THE BOTTOM–Discover Your True Identity Embrace Your Purpose and Develop the Power to Elevate Others
Copyright ©2019 Chad Owen

TULSA, OKLAHOMA

Published by:
Emerge Publishing, LLC
9521B Riverside Parkway, Suite 243
Tulsa, Oklahoma 74137
Phone: 888.407.4447
www.EmergePublishing.com

Library of Congress Cataloging-in-Publication Data

ISBN: 978-1-949758-00-9 Paperback
         978-1-949758-01-6 E-book

BISAC Category:
REL012090   RELIGION / Christian Life / Professional Growth
BUS025000   BUSINESS & ECONOMICS / Entrepreneurship
BUS097000   BUSINESS & ECONOMICS / Workplace Culture

Printed in the United States of America.

TABLE OF CONTENTS

FOREWORD

Write the vision and make it plain on tablets, so he may run
who reads it. (Habakkuk 2:2)

Being asked to write a foreword ranks as one of the higher
honors one can experience and this one is no exception.
When I was approached about it there was great excitement
and numerous thoughts as to what I may say. There were
thoughts such as, who may be reading this book? Will the
author feel honored by what is mentioned? Is there anything I
could say that might grab the attention of both the reader and

the author? It did not take long to realize I was, once again, striving for the top and not for the bottom!

My dear friend, Chad has found a way to communicate a truth that has somehow been forgotten or, at least, largely neglected. He has mastered the way to communicate scriptural truths that he has put to practice in his personal life and has made practical in a manner where anyone can apply it to their own life.

It has been close to twenty years since we started a friendship which has grown into a common bond that mutually encourages one another in faith and family. I have watched first hand a man who has learned to "strive for the bottom" and arrive on top of the world in every aspect of life.

This book you hold in your hands will bring to light eternal principles that you may not find being spoken of much today in our society, especially out of the four walls on the church.

Principles such as: "If anyone is going to follow Me, he must first deny himself..." or "If you want to be great in God's Kingdom then learn to be a servant of all..." and " He must increase and I must decrease."

What has been written in the pages you will begin reading has first been lived by the one who has written them. Therefore, what has been lived and has been written can also be lived by those who will read it.

Scriptural principles put into personal practices can help one achieve what they have only dreamed of before. It is my hopes that your dreams will be achieved and surpassed through the practical truths you find in the pages of this book.

Set before you is a vison made plain. It will give you what you need to run and reach where you desire to be. So read and run. It is as simple as that!

Greg DeVries

Lead Pastor

The Well Family Worship Center

INTRODUCTION

Over the years, I have made many mistakes. Some have cost me a little, and some have cost me a lot. Whether it was relationally, financially, or physically, each mistake had a wounding aspect to them. Because of the mistakes I've made, I've hurt my wife, children, family, friends, and people I have never even known. I wish I would have had more mentors in my life or taken the time to listen to the ones around me.

My father was a product of a hard childhood. He lost both of his parents at a young age and had a very challenging life growing up. I know he meant well, but it felt like my siblings and I were always in competition with him. Over the years, my accomplishments typically resulted with comments such as, *I have done better than that, I have done more than you, I have more accomplishments, you will never make it to where I am*, etc...

Honestly, I wish he would have shared the challenges he had faced, the mistakes he had made, the things he wished he had never done, and helped me go through life learning from the mistakes he had made and what he had done to overcome those mistakes.

I am a father of four children, three girls and then, finally, a boy. I did not care if the fourth child was a boy or girl until I saw him come out. I yelled *It's a boy!* and became overwhelmed with joy at the moment of his birth. I brought my newborn son to my father who was waiting outside the delivery room. Full of joy and fulfillment, I handed him to my father. I expected a *well done, I'm happy for you.* Instead, some of the first words out of his mouth were, *I am still more of a man than you. I have had seven children.* I quickly responded, *No, I am more of a man because I have had all my children with one woman.* My father had been married three times. The point is, even at that precious moment there was competition between us.

Because of my upbringing, I have a very competitive spirit. I have five brothers and one sister (two full brothers, one stepbrother, two half-brothers, and one half-sister). I have spent very little time with some of them because of distance both in miles and relationally. Honestly, I have awesome relationships with my two full brothers. We still talk and make a point to see each other consistently, even though we all live in different states. Both are very successful in business and are great fathers and husbands. Unfortunately, it's not the same with my other brothers and sister. I wish it were, but it is not; someday we will reconnect.

What would it have been like to have a relationship with my father who thrived on him pushing me upward, forward and beyond what he had ever accomplished? I believe I am what I am because I saw certain things in my father that I did not want to be. I want to be clear, my father has been deceased for some time now, and I have no hard feelings or unforgiveness toward him. I loved him very much and truly believe he tried his best in raising us. When he passed, I mourned for what could have been rather than what was. This sense of loss and competition is not gender specific. Mothers and daughters may experience this as well. I have seen many mothers in competition with their daughters, and it can be very damaging and unhealthy from a relational standpoint.

I have raised four children who all love Jesus. My two oldest are married to awesome men of God. I want to be a father and mentor who thrives on and celebrates the success and advancement of others. I want the people I mentor to go far beyond where I have ever been. Over the course of this book, I will share many stories, examples, and lessons I have learned over the years.

I consider myself very successful in being a son, husband, father, friend, mentor, and businessman, but I have a very long way to go. I believe there will never be an *I have arrived* moment. We can always be better, learn more, and improve the environment around us. Life is about succeeding in all areas and continually **Striving for the Bottom**. I will go into more detail about what this means. I don't meet many people who are **Striving for the Bottom**, but by the time you're finished reading this book, I pray that the bottom is your goal.

———

CHAPTER 1

YOUR GREATEST ENEMY

I have helped, counseled, mentored, and fathered many people and will continue to do so until my living accommodation is upgraded to Heaven. Here are a few common questions that I've consistently been asked over the years:

What is my purpose?

Why am I here?

What am I supposed to accomplish in life?

How do I find this out?

How do I get started?

I'm sure many of us have asked these same questions at some point in our lives. It's normal and expected to ask these questions. We all want to feel like we've accomplished something and made a difference while living on this little blue ball we call Earth. Even the most rebellious people I've met are living for a purpose, it's just a misdirected and misguided focus. They are still fulfilling a purpose, but rebellion is usually a reaction to misdirected guidance during childhood. I served in youth ministry for years and used to get extremely upset with parents who abused their children physically or emotionally.

The Lord had a moment with me one day when I wanted to beat the living daylights out of a father who would consistently go home drunk and abuse his family. I heard the Lord ask me, *why do you think this abusive man is like that?*

In anger, I responded *because he is a jerk and deserves to be beaten.* The Lord told me, *No, his father was the same way, and he has not been taught who he is and whose he is. He is a reflection and product of his earthly father. He is projecting the image he was made in.*

I lead a discipleship group called Daddy Hugs which is a group of younger ladies including my wife and three daughters. For one of our gatherings, I asked the Holy Spirit what

I should talk about, and He told me, *show them their greatest enemy and the most destructive tool used against them.* I was then given a prop and an illustration to use.

This discipleship group meets at our house, and the ladies typically gather on our huge sectional couch. This particular gathering, every inch of our couch was utilized with ladies snuggled shoulder to shoulder. Quite the opposite of my men's discipleship group, Mighty Men, which has a "no touchy" rule. With all the ladies sitting in front of me, I pulled the sheet off my prop, revealing a full-length mirror. I then shared what the Holy Spirit revealed to me. The mirror is not the enemy; it's what you let the mirror say about you that is dangerous.

You see, the mirror will always reflect what is in front of it. Only you can say what the mirror is saying. You determine what it says.

One of the major problems with the power of the mirror is that it is greatly magnified by what a mother or father has or has not said. It can also have power based on the environment you have allowed yourself to be in. I will go into more depth on this topic in the chapter covering identity.

Comparing ourselves to others is a killer of identity and purpose.

> We were born originals, each of us a masterpiece.
> It is important we do not die a copy or cheap replica.

Satan does not want us to know who we are, whose we are, or what we are put on this planet for. I've heard this saying many times: the two most important days in our lives are the day we were born, and the day we find out why. Finding the *why* is an important revelation in striving for the bottom.

QUESTIONS:

➤ What have you allowed the mirror to say about you?

_____

_____

_____

_____

_____

_____

_____

➤ What have you said to others that would magnify what the mirror says to them? Both good and bad.

Good _____

_____

_____

_____

_____

_____

_____

_____

Bad _____

_____

_____

_____

_____

_____

_____

_____

CHAPTER 2

IT'S REAL TO THE PUPPY

Before we go into the guts and soul of this book, I want to reveal another important thing we need to do to discover our own identity and purpose. This entire book has been birthed from an incredible passion of mine. I love helping people find out the *why* in life. As we are finding the why in our own life or trying to help others find theirs, we tend to minimize experiences and circumstances, thinking of them as no big deal or something that shouldn't have knocked us down so easily. I will give you a couple of examples of how this has happened to me.

When my daughter was twelve years old, she had a massive brain aneurysm and brain bleed. She was on life support for seven days, in the ICU for eleven days, and in the hospital for a total of forty-three days. The whole story will be for another book in the future.

My daughter, Ariel, had to have five brain surgeries. We had a remarkable surgeon, but he could have used a more sensitive approach. I've learned over the years that people with extraordinarily tough jobs often remove the emotion from their job to avoid a meltdown in the midst of their performance. This surgeon had operated on people who I am sure ended up dying or not recovering well, so I understood his demeanor.

When Ariel was first hospitalized, the surgeon informed us of how incredibly rare it was for a twelve-year-old girl to have a bleed in the brain (brain hemorrhage) like this. The odds of my little girl having this condition were about one in a million. Well as you can imagine, that didn't bring us much comfort as parents. I said to the doctor, *I appreciate your statistics, but when you are one of the statistics, it compounds the emotions because you start to question why God would "let" your daughter be one of them.*

After four or so attempts to stop the bleeding in her brain with super glue injections, the doctor decided an aggressive surgery was the only answer. With all logic and zero emotion, he explained in a very matter of fact way, *we must cut the skin above the hairline of her scalp, cut through the skull and separate the upper and lower brain (layman's terms), and pull out the bad veins.* I remember telling him, *Doc, I know you are trying to explain this to us, but this is our daughter and it's hard for us to hear what's being done to her.*

Because he had performed so many of these procedures, she was just another surgery, not a person. As I stated, this doctor was awesome and was a huge part of our daughter surviving through this. I won't leave you hanging though. Ariel did have to relearn how to walk, talk, eat, and swallow, but is now healthy and happily married!

Another example of minimizing experiences happened when I was about sixteen years old. I thought I had fallen in love with a girl until she broke up with me, ripped my heart out, set it on fire, ran over it, threw it in reverse, and backed over it. I may be over-dramatizing a little, but most of us remember a boy or girl in our life who made us feel this way.

Well, I was home, heartbroken, crying in my bedroom when my dad walked in. He asked, *What's the matter?* I told him that a girl ripped my heart out and his response was, *don't worry, it was only puppy love.* I remember quickly responding, *Yeah, but it's real to the puppy!*

As time passed, I married the woman of my dreams, and we had a few children of our own. One afternoon my daughters were playing with Barbie, and the doll's head flew off! My girls started to cry. I came in, put Barbie's head back on, and the drama was over. You see, at the time, it was a major situation to them. To me, it was no big deal. I just popped Barbie's head back on. For them, it was a "Real to the Puppy" moment. As we go through life, we need to realize the "Real to the Puppy" moments in our own lives and the lives of those around us. This will help us to be more compassionate to others.

I believe Jesus was a master at the "Real to the Puppy" moments. In the Bible, when others are screaming to the desperate people, *it's not a big deal, don't bother Him, you are a waste of His time,* Jesus stopped and had compassion for their life and circumstances. Jesus paused to take time out for the "Real to the Puppy" moments in people's lives. Before we progress to the next chapter, we need to address some of these moments we've experienced so we can approach others with the same compassion, always remembering how Jesus responded.

QUESTIONS:

➢ What is a moment where you removed your emotion from a circumstance and didn't have the emotionally-based response you should have had?

_____

_____

_____

_____

_____

_____

_____

➢ What was a "Real to the Puppy" moment for you and
   how did you handle it?

_____

_____

_____

_____

_____

_____

_____

➢ What can you do to make sure you have more compassion for other people's circumstances?

_____

_____

_____

_____

_____

_____

_____

CHAPTER 3

WHO AND WHOSE
FINDING YOUR IDENTITY
(BEING A SON OR DAUGHTER OF GOD)

DEFINITION OF IDENTITY

plural **identities**

: sameness of essential or generic character in different instances

: sameness in all that constitutes the objective reality of a thing

: the distinguishing character or personality of an individual

: the relation established by psychological identification

: the condition of being the same with something described or asserted establish the identity of stolen goods

: an equation that is satisfied for all values of the symbols

One of the first questions I ask anyone I'm mentoring is, *what is your identity?* I'm amazed at the answers I've received over the years. The majority of people, probably 9 out of 10, don't know what their true identity is. They will typically say mother, father, mechanic, friend, brother, husband, wife, etc. To me, none of these answers is your true identity; they are what you *do*. Let me explain.

I believe our identity is something that can never change. It is who we are to the very core. Our identity is something that is given to us by God and can never change, no matter what. When we base our identity on something that can change, then we then must rediscover our identity if this change occurs. If my identity is a husband and my wife passes away, I am no longer a husband. Therefore, I have lost my identity. Now, not only do I have to deal with losing my spouse, but I also must refigure who I am. I work with retirees and often encounter this exact scenario. A spouse passes away, and the widow or widower has now lost their identity because it was rooted in their spouse. The same applies to losing a child, job, sibling, etc. I don't believe our identity should be based off of something that can change.

Please hear me out. My wife struggled with her true identity at a time in her life when our children were very young. As life progresses, most mothers and fathers can relate to this. I remember one day my wife said in a frustrated tone, clearly searching for who she is, *I am a mother and a wife, but I do not feel like I know who I am.* Now anyone who knows my wife knows that she is incredibly selfless, pure, loving, and thoughtful. She is constantly loving and blessing others, making them feel loved and special. When she expressed, *I don't know who I am*, like a dodo I replied, *You are my wife and the mother of our children! How do you not see that?*

You see, at that time, I didn't understand true identity. My wife, Leilani, needed to be more than a mother, wife, friend, or any other action-based identity. Being a wife, mother, friend, sister, brother, CEO, or business owner is great, but these alone will never provide a true sense of identity. These action-based identities will never be enough. An action-based identity is a purpose, not who you are. We will discuss purpose in the next chapter.

Our identity is something that needs to be unshakable, never changing. Our identity is the foundation of who we are, upon which everything else in our life is built. When you look at the dictionary definition of identity at the beginning of this chapter, I'd argue that it misses the mark. There is only one identity that can never be changed, the one that was given to us before we were born. It came from the Creator Himself.

Here it is: **You are a child of God, a son or daughter of the Creator of all, a prince or princess to the King of kings. This identity can never change.**

Being a husband, wife, parent, boss, or sibling are all things that can change due to life circumstances or choices we make. As I pointed out earlier, if Leilani passed away, I would no longer be a husband. If I'm a boss and I get fired, I am no longer a boss. If I have one sibling and they pass away, I am no longer a sibling. I think you get my point. Being a child of God can never be given or taken away. It is an eternal title (identity) that has been woven into our very DNA. It is unshakable. Even if you don't claim it, it will not change.

Let me explain it another way. Let's say you have a toaster, a blender, and a crock pot in front of you. What is their identity? Well, it's pretty simple. Their identity is a toaster, blender, and crock pot. That will not change. Each one is designed to do something different. What they are designed to do is different from what they are. What they do is their purpose. How do you find out what their purpose is? You have to plug them in! The toaster can say it's a blender, but when you plug it in, it will not blend things, it will only toast.

Distinguishing the difference between identity and purpose is essential. You will never find a purpose that will fulfill you until you discover your true identity. Your identity is the foundation upon which you build all aspects and areas of your life and future.

It's a person's state of awareness about their identity at any given moment that decrees their behavior and therefore their results. When you know your God-given identity, you will respond rather than react.

You will never outperform your self-image. You need to know who you are and why you exist to make the most impact! Your identity lets you walk in the confidence of who made you. Your self-image (identity) can and does affect the way you impact others. You cannot fully help someone believe in who they are if you don't believe in who you are.

The best way to change someone's behavior is to change their beliefs about themselves. Therefore, helping

someone find their identity and value is so
important. The image we see will determine what we can do
and what we will see in others. God's Word is
the reflection we need to see about ourselves.

We must remember, satan is the greatest identity thief in history and has been stealing people's identity long before credit cards and social security numbers came into existence. Satan does not want you to discover or walk in your true identity. Once you truly recognize that you are of Royal blood and have the authority of the King, satan becomes a defeated, powerless foe.

Everything boils down to knowing who you are and whose you are. Ask the Holy Spirit to saturate you with His Love and to speak who you are to the Creator of the universe. Be open and accepting to being a son or daughter. Believe that that alone is enough, and you are worthy of that title. Nothing you've ever done will or can disqualify you from being a son or daughter of God.

Below is an example of what I've written for my own identity. I've left some space for you to write your own as well. Write down your identity and then below that put what our Father says about you. What do God's Word and the Holy

Spirit speak over you? As confirmation, write Scriptures that solidify what He says about you. In the next chapter, we will discover how to find your purpose.

Prayer: *Father, Holy Spirit, fill me with the identity You have for me. Speak to me, remind me, and whisper to me in tough times who I am to You. Help me walk in my identity, sharing Your Love with others at all times. Help me be an example to others, so they see the identity You have given me and that they too will find theirs.*

PERSONAL EXAMPLE OF IDENTITY:

- Identity – I am a child of God and a prince to the King of kings. I am a warrior for the Kingdom, walking with all the authority and power of my Father. I will not fail or ever be defeated! I have already won through the victory that my Jesus attained at the cross.
- What does God say about me?
  i.   I am a child of God – Galatians 3:26
  ii. He loves me – Romans 8:37-39
  iii. I am made in His image – Genesis 1:26

This is what God has spoken to me about my personal identity. Take some time to answer the questions below:

MY PERSONAL STATEMENT OF IDENTITY:

_____

_____

_____

_____

_____

_____

QUESTIONS:

What does God, the Creator of the Universe, say about me and which Scriptures solidify it?

➤ What He says about me:

_____

_____

_____

_____

_____

_____

Scripture _____

➤ What He says about me:

_____

_____

_____

_____

_____

_____

Scripture _____

➤ What He says about me:

_____

_____

_____

_____

_____

_____

Scripture _____

➤ What He says about me:

_____

_____

_____

_____

_____

Scripture _____

CHAPTER 4

THE WHAT AND WHY
DISCOVERING YOUR PURPOSE
(WHAT ARE YOU MADE FOR, DESIGNED FOR?)

DEFINITION OF PURPOSE

: something set up as an object or end to be attained

: a subject under discussion or action in the course of execution

I pray that by this point you have truly found your identity and believe what God says about you and who you are called to be. Now for the next step. What is your purpose in life? What are you made for? This is where accomplishment and fulfillment of your identity come into play. Your purpose is the first floor built upon the foundation of your identity. Here is an example of mine:

STRUCTURE	FLOORS
FLOOR 6	I am an Icebreaker
FLOOR 5	I am the Captain
FLOOR 4	I am the Top Cup
FLOOR 3	I am a Watchman
FLOOR 2	I am a Father
FLOOR 1	I am a Husband
FOUNDATION	Son of God

The purpose *floors* can be changed at any time. Obviously, being a spouse and parent are meant to be there for as long as you live. But the other purpose floors can change, be added to, or removed at any given time in one's life. As we grow and mature, the purposes in our life will change and continue developing. When you steward your purpose well, God will give you more and more responsibility. And your impact for the Kingdom will increase just as Scripture states in the parable of the talents.

There needs to be an importance placed on the order of your purposes. My first floor is as a husband. If you are married, being a spouse should be the first floor. If we don't focus on the purpose of being a Godly spouse, we cannot build any higher without a threat of the building collapsing in the future. Once the spouse floor is established, you can build the parental floor. This floor is the next level of importance. If I'm a good spouse but a poor father, anything I build above the parental floor may collapse the building as well. As I said previously, *you are born an original, don't die a copy.* Do not compare your building to anyone else's. To balance this statement, I believe it is wise to lean on the counsel of mentors to help you establish this building of life. It's better to have wise engineers helping you build so that you will face less structural issues or collapse in the future. Now, how do you discover your purpose?

Let's go back to the end of Chapter 3. Remember the toaster, blender, and crock pot in front of you? What is their identity? Well, it's pretty simple. Their identity is toaster, blender, and crock pot. These will not change. Each one is designed to do something different. What they are designed to do is different from what they are. What they do is also known as their purpose. How do you find out what their purpose is? You must plug them in! The toaster can say it's a blender, but when you plug it in, it won't blend things, it will only toast. Therefore, distinguishing the difference between identity and purpose is critical.

Plugging yourself in is asking the Holy Spirit to show you what He designed you to do. You must plug into the source. When we read the Bible, it's full of the purposes we were made for. It is important to find out which ones we were designed for. Scripture tells it like this:

1 CORINTHIANS 12:14-27 NIV

[14] Even so the body is not made up of one part but of many. [15] Now if the foot should say, "Because I am not a hand, I do not belong to the body," it would not for that reason stop being part of the body. [16] And if the ear should say, "Because I am not an eye, I do not belong to the body," it would not for that reason stop being part of the body. [17] If the whole body were an eye, where would the sense of hearing be? If the whole body were an ear, where would the sense of smell be? [18] But in fact God has placed

the parts in the body, every one of them, just as he wanted them to be. ¹⁹ If they were all one part, where would the body be? ²⁰ As it is, there are many parts, but one body. ²¹ The eye cannot say to the hand, "I don't need you!" And the head cannot say to the feet, "I don't need you!" ²² On the contrary, those parts of the body that seem to be weaker are indispensable, ²³ and the parts that we think are less honorable we treat with special honor. And the parts that are unpresentable are treated with special modesty, ²⁴ while our presentable parts need no special treatment. But God has put the body together, giving greater honor to the parts that lacked it, ²⁵ so that there should be no division in the body, but that its parts should have equal concern for each other. ²⁶ If one part suffers, every part suffers with it; if one part is honored, every part rejoices with it. ²⁷ Now you are the body of Christ, and each one of you is a part of it.

I look at each part of the body of Christ as a purpose we are to fulfill. We all have purposes to advance the Kingdom of God, and no one's purpose is more important than anyone else's. Let me say that again. No one's purpose is greater than another's if it's given to you by God. We all have a part in the body, and all serve a purpose. Do not compare yours to another's. Comparison is a killer of your purpose.

You can always tell when a person discovers their purpose. They become unstoppable and are not moved by their circumstances. A person with a purpose will not let a situation control them. They control their circumstances by how they respond. If you recall from earlier, when we are rooted in our true identity, we respond rather than react to our circumstances. If you know your purpose is from God, then a circumstance, which is temporal, will not change your purpose.

How do you discover your purpose? How can you determine if it's from God? Kingdom purpose develops Kingdom results. Matthew 6:33 states, "Seek ye first the Kingdom of God and all these things shall be added unto you." How do you tell the difference between Kingdom purpose and others? Kingdom purpose always has an eternal impact. Every other purpose has temporary results. In the next chapter, we will discover how to walk in and succeed in your purpose by attaining knowledge.

Prayer: *Father, show me Your heart for my life and help me to find and fulfill my purpose and calling. Help me to represent You* *at all times and in all places. Fill me with the Holy Spirit's focus on Your will in my life.*

PERSONAL EXAMPLE STATEMENTS FOR PURPOSE:

- **I am a Husband** who will always love, appreciate, and admire the beauty my wife has inside and out. I will protect her with my life, ready to lay it down for her at any given time. I will do my best to represent Jesus for her as He is for us.

- **I am a Father** bringing the Father's love and grace for my children and children's children. I am a father to the fatherless, bringing the adoptive Spirit of our Heavenly Father.

- **I am a Watchman**, keeping guard and looking out for those who intend to harm the helpless and hurting. I see into the physical and spiritual realms, protecting others from the attacks of the enemy.

- **I am the Top Cup** being poured into, overflowing with the Lord's abundant heart, to fill others with such a force that it splashes everywhere with passion and purpose.

- **I am the Captain** of an oil tanker, with a crew that has the same dreams and desires to provide resources for the Kingdom! I cannot take credit for the ship or the resources it carries because it all belongs to the Lord. My only job is to get the resources from point A to B, teaching the crew the knowledge, wisdom, and revelation to one day be the captain of their own fleets.

- **I am an Icebreaker** pushing forward with all force, clearing a path for others to bring their resources. I will not be intimidated by the thickness of any ice that is in front of me for the weight of the Father is with me. When I am weak and tired, He is strong and wide awake.

I have given you an example of what I have written for my purpose. Below that, I have left some space for you to write your own. Write down your purpose or purposes and then list what our Father has called you to do. What do the Holy Spirit and God's Word speak over you?

MY PERSONAL STATEMENT(S) FOR PURPOSE:

➤ I am a(n) _____

_____

_____

_____

_____

_____

➤ I am a(n) _____

_____

_____

_____

_____

_____

➤ I am a(n) _____

_____

_____

_____

_____

_____

➢ I am a(n) _____

_____

_____

_____

_____

_____

_____

➢ I am a(n) _____

_____

_____

_____

_____

_____

_____

➢ I am a(n) _____

_____

_____

_____

_____

_____

_____

CHAPTER 5

THE STARTING POINT
ATTAINING KNOWLEDGE

DEFINITION OF KNOWLEDGE

: the fact or condition of knowing something with familiarity gained through experience

: acquaintance with or understanding of science, art, or technique

: the fact or condition of being aware of something

: the range of one's information or understanding answered to the best of my *knowledge*

: the circumstance or condition of apprehending truth or fact through reasoning

: the fact or condition of having information or of being learned: a person of unusual *knowledge*

: the sum of what is known: the body of truth, information, and principles acquired by humankind

Hopefully, you now have a better idea of your identity and are starting to understand your purpose. Once you start to understand what your purpose is, you must attain the knowledge for these purposes. Lack of knowledge creates some of the greatest gaps in the application of one's purpose. I have met many individuals who know their purpose and have been spoken into by many people. But they are not willing to take the steps to attain knowledge so they can fulfill their purpose.

Hosea 4:6 says "My people are destroyed for a lack of knowledge."

I believe many lives are destroyed because people are too lazy, unmotivated, or just plain rebellious, not wanting to take the time to learn.

As I stated in the previous chapter, once we establish our identity and purpose, we can begin to build the next floor which is knowledge. As I wrote this book, the Lord said, *the floor of knowledge can have ceilings as high as the eye can see. Knowledge is unlimited to those who seek it.*

STRUCTURE	FLOORS
FLOOR 7	KNOWLEDGE
FLOOR 6	PURPOSE
FLOOR 5	PURPOSE
FLOOR 4	PURPOSE
FLOOR 3	PURPOSE
FLOOR 2	PURPOSE
FLOOR 1	PURPOSE
FOUNDATION	IDENTITY

There are many ways to attain knowledge. Here are some of the most common:

- **Become a student:**
  - I love learning from others who are wiser and more experienced than me. One of the dumbest things I hear people say is, "I need to learn for myself and make the mistakes myself." I would much rather learn from the mistakes of others, so I don't have to waste time going through the same trials and errors. Depending on what you are learning,

mistakes can be very expensive! I have made mistakes that have cost me upward of six figures. I am tired of the pain I've experienced for myself and others around me when making these mistakes. I would rather make mistakes forging new territory than make a mistake that someone else has already made.

- I'm not a huge fan of college unless you are going for a degree or pursuing a field that requires a degree. I believe college nowadays is full of extreme professors who spew their political opinions as fact. It also does not make sense that you have to take the basic courses that you most likely completed in high school. College and universities can also become a breeding ground for immorality. That being said, at the time of this book, three out of four of my children have graduated or are in college. I make sure they don't have student debt of any sort, and I've been able to father them heavily, combating the barrage of attacks on their identity and purpose. I say all of this because the wrong knowledge can destroy the direction and call on someone's life. Parents, it's so critical to keep your children close to you during the first twenty-five years of their lives. The part of the brain that processes long-term decisions is not fully developed until around age twenty-five. Call it overprotective, overparenting, or whatever you want. As a parent, I've met many people whose children lost their minds during their high school and college years.

- **Read or listen to books:**
  - I've only read two to three physical books in my life, but I've listened to more than I can even count. When I read, I don't retain information as well as when I listen. For this reason, my books are available in all formats. There are many benefits to reading such as:
    - Increased focus
    - Perspective
    - Insight
    - Inner reflection
    - Stimulates creativity

- ☐ Improved memory retention
- ☐ And many more benefits.
- I cannot recall ever meeting anyone with major success who doesn't read. Successful people are typically like sponges, soaking up as much knowledge as they can.
- And of course, if you want to know how a product works and functions, you read the owner's manual. The Bible is the written Word of God and has every bit of information we need to know when it's revealed through the Holy Spirit. We will talk about revelation in the chapters to come.

- **Practice:**
  - Just doing something over and over again until you get it right can work as well. Just like when you practiced tying your shoelaces, riding a bike, or driving a car. All of these abilities took practice until you had the knowledge to do what you were trying to do. It's important to be taught by someone who's experienced in what you want to learn so you don't waste time practicing the wrong way.

- **Stepping up and out:**
  - When you take a leap of faith or are thrown into a new place of responsibility, you will be forced to attain knowledge if you ever hope to succeed.
- **Listen and observe:**
  - I believe there's a reason why God gave us two ears, two eyes, and one mouth. Attaining knowledge can be as simple as watching and listening to others while keeping our mouths shut. Many times, when I was young, I would sit in my grandfather's workshop and listen to him tell me what he was doing and watch to see how he would do it. As you can imagine, as a little boy, my mind had a billion questions. I would get excited when my grandfather would look at me and ask if I'd like to help. It made me feel really important. In a way, I feel that this is how our Heavenly Father operates. We need to listen and observe the Word of God and wait for Him to look at us and ask if we want to help. I love it when He asks me this!

We must be careful about the type of knowledge we are soaking in as well. I have met many people who have bathed in knowledge that reek of arrogance and pride. We will never attain enough knowledge to be superior or better than anyone. If we go back to the blender analogy, what would happen if you threw large metal, nuts, bolts, and washers into it? You would dull all the blades and eventually it would become useless and broken. Knowledge in the wrong form can do the same thing to our inner being. Knowledge only becomes powerful when introduced and combined with wisdom. In the next chapter, we will go through the process of attaining wisdom.

Prayer: *Father, show me the right ways to attain the knowledge that helps me succeed in fulfilling my purpose. Protect me from deceptive teachings and deceptive teachers. Allow my brain and neural pathways to absorb and soak in the right knowledge and retain it for future needs. Thank You that I have the mind of Christ and I can do all things through Jesus!*

PERSONAL EXAMPLE STATEMENT FOR KNOWLEDGE:

I will daily seek to pull in knowledge from all sources to fulfill the purpose God has called me to do. As I attain knowledge for my current level, I will pursue even more as I continue to go from promotion to promotion.

I've given you an example of what I've done and continue to do to attain knowledge. Below that, I have left some space for you to write the ways you will attain knowledge and some goals to set for yourself to achieve this knowledge.

MY PERSONAL STATEMENT FOR KNOWLEDGE:

_____

_____

_____

_____

_____

_____

_____

QUESTIONS:

➢ Which ways listed above do I retain knowledge the best?

_____

_____

_____

_____

_____

➢ What goal am I going to set and finish in the next month to grow my knowledge to walk in my purpose?

_____

_____

_____

_____

_____

➢ How many books will I read/listen to in the next year and which ones?

_____

_____

_____

_____

_____

CHAPTER 6

SEEKING MORE

PURSUING WISDOM

DEFINITION OF WISDOM

: ability to discern inner qualities and relationships

: good sense

: generally accepted belief

: accumulated philosophical or scientific learning

: a wise attitude, belief, or course of action

: the teachings of the ancient wise men

Wisdom can be very tricky to who we are and how we believe. King Solomon, one of the wisest people to ever live showed us that wisdom could be both a blessing and a curse in a sense. Wisdom gave him fame and fortune but was not enough to keep him from marrying a foreign woman who ended up being one of the major problems during his reign. I am often asked, how do you attain wisdom? My first response is always, Read the book of Proverbs. Proverbs is a book in the Bible that has 31 chapters. It's advised to read a chapter a day and repeat this for the rest of your life. King Solomon could have had anything he wanted. Scripture says it like this:

1 KINGS 3:1-15

Solomon made an alliance with Pharaoh king of Egypt and married his daughter. He brought her to the City of David until he finished building his palace and the temple of the LORD, and the wall around Jerusalem. ² The people, however, were still sacrificing at the high places, because a temple had not yet been built for the Name of the LORD. ³ Solomon showed his love for the LORD by walking according to the instructions given him by his father David, except that he offered sacrifices and burned incense on the high places. ⁴ The king went to Gibeon to offer sacrifices, for that was the most important high place, and Solomon offered a thousand burnt offerings on that altar. ⁵ At Gibeon the LORD appeared to Solomon during the night in a dream, and God said, "Ask for whatever you want me to give you." ⁶ Solomon answered, "You have shown great kindness to your servant, my father David, because he was faithful to you and righteous and upright in heart. You have continued this great kindness to him and have given him a son to sit on his throne this very day. ⁷ "Now, LORD my God, you have made your servant king in place of my father David. But I am only a little child and do not know how to carry out my duties. ⁸ Your servant is here among the people you have chosen, a great people, too numerous to count or number. ⁹ So give your servant a discerning heart to govern your people and to distinguish between right and wrong. For who is able to govern this great people of yours?" ¹⁰ The Lord was pleased that Solomon had asked for this. ¹¹ So God said to him, "Since you have asked for this and not for long life or wealth for yourself, nor have asked for the death of your enemies but for discernment in administering justice, ^{12} I will do what you have asked. I will give you a wise and discerning heart, so that there will never have been anyone like you, nor will there ever be. ^{13} Moreover, I will give you what you have not asked for—both wealth and honor—so that in your lifetime you will have no equal among kings. ^{14} And if you walk in obedience to me and keep my decrees and commands as David your father did, I will give you a long life." ^{15} Then Solomon awoke—and he realized it had been a dream. He returned to Jerusalem, stood before the ark of the Lord's covenant and sacrificed burnt offerings and fellowship offerings. Then he gave a feast for all his court.

You see, King Solomon could have asked for and received anything he wanted. God's response is typical of His character. When we ask for something to help others rather than fulfill our selfish desires, He responds extravagantly.

1 Kings 4:29-34 says it like this:

> ^{29} God gave Solomon wisdom and very great insight, and a breadth of understanding as measureless as the sand on the seashore. ^{30} Solomon's wisdom was greater than the

wisdom of all the people of the East and greater than all the wisdom of Egypt. ³¹ He was wiser than anyone else, including Ethan the Ezrahite—wiser than Heman, Kalkol, and Darda, the sons of Mahol. And his fame spread to all the surrounding nations. ³² He spoke three thousand proverbs, and his songs numbered a thousand and five. ³³ He spoke about plant life, from the cedar of Lebanon to the hyssop that grows out of walls. He also spoke about animals and birds, reptiles and fish. ³⁴ From all nations, people came to listen to Solomon's wisdom, sent by all the kings of the world, who had heard of his wisdom.

King Solomon had a very influential position in the world. Rulers throughout the world sought his wisdom. Wisdom shouted King Solomon's name throughout the world. Here's what one of the greatest rulers of that time, the Queen of Sheba, said about King Solomon. Here's how it is written in 1 Kings 10:1-9:

¹When the queen of Sheba heard about the fame of Solomon and his relationship to the LORD; she came to test Solomon with hard questions. ² Arriving at Jerusalem with a very great caravan—with camels carrying spices,

large quantities of gold, and precious stones—she came to Solomon and talked with him about all that she had on her mind. ³ Solomon answered all her questions; nothing was too hard for the king to explain to her. ⁴ When the queen of Sheba saw all the wisdom of Solomon and the palace he had built, ⁵ the food on his table, the seating of his officials, the attending servants in their robes, his cupbearers, and the burnt offerings he made at the temple of the LORD, she was overwhelmed. ⁶ She said to the king, "The report I heard in my own country about your achievements and your wisdom is true. ⁷ But I did not believe these things until I came and saw with my own eyes. Indeed, not even half was told me; in wisdom and wealth, you have far exceeded the report I heard. ⁸ How happy your people must be! How happy your officials, who continually stand before you and hear your wisdom! ⁹ Praise be to the LORD your God, who has delighted in you and placed you on the throne of Israel. Because of the LORD's eternal love for Israel, he has made you king to maintain justice and righteousness."

I find it interesting that wealth was drawn to wisdom and generosity as referred to in 1 Kings 10:10-13:

[10] And she gave the king 120 talents of gold, large quantities of spices, and precious stones. Never again were so many spices brought in as those the queen of Sheba gave to King Solomon. [11] (Hiram's ships brought gold from Ophir, and from there they brought great cargoes of almugwood and precious stones. [12] The king used the almug wood to make supports for the temple of the Lord and for the royal palace, and to make harps and lyres for the musicians. So much almugwood has never been imported or seen since that day.) [13] King Solomon gave the queen of Sheba all she desired and asked for, besides what he had given her out of his royal bounty. Then she left and returned with her retinue to her own country.

I am always fascinated with biblical principles in action. When we live our lives the way God intended and designed us to, we become well-oiled machines, producing His Goodness all over the world!

With all that said, I believe there is something even greater than wisdom, and I will go over that in the next chapter.

If we look at the building model where we started, we started with the foundation of identity and the first floors of our purpose. We then have to attain and seek knowledge to fulfill and learn how to live out our purpose. Once we have knowledge, it's critical to seek out and soak in wisdom. The best way to attain wisdom is seeking it through God's Word. I've also attained much wisdom through the counsel of Godly people in my life, people filled with the Holy Spirit. Wisdom is the practical application of knowledge. Therefore, wisdom is the next floor above knowledge.

STRUCTURE	FLOORS
FLOOR 8	WISDOM
FLOOR 7	KNOWLEDGE
FLOOR 6	PURPOSE
FLOOR 5	PURPOSE
FLOOR 4	PURPOSE
FLOOR 3	PURPOSE
FLOOR 2	PURPOSE
FLOOR 1	PURPOSE
FOUNDATION	IDENTITY

As you can see, the building is getting bigger and taller. Only in the Kingdom and with God's help can we expand the size of the building both in width and height without tearing it down and starting all over again. God has designed His influence and Being to be continuously expanding. Since He lives in us, we can do the same. Unlike knowledge, wisdom comes with something that demands from you. Knowledge by itself can be selfish. Wisdom demands flexibility and a willingness to grow. Wisdom can transform knowledge into something beautiful and productive. Living in God's wisdom allows Heavenly blessings to move into action.

As I've hinted to you a few times in this chapter, wisdom alone is not enough. Even with all his wisdom, King Solomon seemed to implode near the end of his life. He wrote a book called Ecclesiastes that reveals wisdom, mixed with sorrow and regret. It appears to me that King Solomon didn't know his Father very well. I honestly don't see how you could when you have as many wives and concubines as he did. His son and heir Rehoboam was a mess!

In my opinion, there is something far greater than wisdom. It is divine and Heaven-sent. What I'll be covering in the next chapter combines identity, purpose, knowledge, and wisdom, which can create an unstoppable forward progression and insight.

Prayer: *Father, show me the right way to apply my wisdom to the knowledge I have sought out. I pray for wisdom that is overflowing and endless; the wisdom that is far beyond me, that when people look at what I know, they'll see it is You and Your favor in me that shines.*

PERSONAL EXAMPLE STATEMENT FOR WISDOM:

I will seek God's Word and the counsel of elders and experts in the area I'm called to be in. I will be open to correction and guidance with a humble and willing heart.

I've given you an example of what I've done and continue to do for attaining wisdom. Below that, I've left some space for you to write the ways you will attain wisdom and some goals you'll set for yourself to achieve this:

MY PERSONAL STATEMENT FOR WISDOM:

_____

_____

_____

_____

_____

_____

_____

QUESTIONS:

➤ How am I going to seek out wisdom and what resources will I use?

_____

_____

_____

_____

_____

_____

_____

➤ Who am I going to reach out to for counsel and wisdom?

_____

_____

_____

_____

_____

_____

CHAPTER 7

KNOWING OF THE UNKNOWN

SEEKING REVELATION

DEFINITION OF REVELATION

: an act of revealing or communicating divine truth

: something that is revealed by God to humans

: an act of revealing to view or making known

: something that is revealed; *especially*: an enlightening or astonishing disclosure shocking *revelations*

: a pleasant, often enlightening surprise: her talent was a *revelation*

I knew before I started writing this book that this would be one of my favorite chapters. Revelation is the Holy Spirit's application of knowledge and wisdom. Revelation is God-breathed, Heaven-sent, and full of who God is. I attribute a huge part of my success in life to the many revelations I've received from God. I operate in the office of a prophet in both personal and business realms. Revelation from God is for anyone who wants it and has His heart. With revelation comes the power of living a prophetic lifestyle.

JOEL 2:28-29

"Then, after doing all those things, I will pour out my Spirit upon all people. Your sons and daughters will prophesy. Your old men will dream dreams, and your young men will see visions. In those days I will pour out my Spirit even on servants—men and women alike."

I've had people over the years come up and ask me massive questions with enormous weight about major business decisions. If it weren't for the revelation of the Holy Spirit, I wouldn't dare answer or advise on anything like this because of the consequences of getting it wrong. The same would apply to a personal question such as, *what should I do for a career? Which college should I pick? Is this person good for me?* You know, lightweight stuff like that. Only through revelation from the Holy Spirit should you advise on these kinds of matters.

I couldn't be where I am today without revelation. You see, I don't have an official college degree or any fancy titles. Yet, I own multiple businesses that have made many millions of dollars over the years. I have an awesome marriage of over 25 years to a beautiful woman, and I have four world-changing children who love and follow Jesus. The two oldest have married men that every father dreams their daughters would marry; men of God who treat them with love, admiration, appreciation, and honor. I am living the dream. I could never have achieved any of this, at this magnitude, without the revelation of the Holy Spirit. Now, here is another balancing statement. Just because I'm living the dream doesn't mean everything is perfect and without major challenges. I've endured many challenges that have made me crumble to my knees and even knocked me out at times.

In those difficult times, it's always the Holy Spirit who whispers and at times shouts, *GET UP! Shake it off, and get back in the game!* No amount of knowledge or wisdom can get you going again in these moments of life like revelation can.

As we look at the building of **Striving for the Bottom**, the Lord showed me the revelation floor as an open-air floor that surrounds the environment in and around the building. Revelation is an atrium because revelation needs to be free and open, constantly surrounding all areas of our life. Revelation creates an atmosphere that allows the building to live in a Heavenly environment.

R		STRUCTURE	FLOORS	
E ←		OPEN ATRIUM	REVELATION	
V		FLOOR 8	WISDOM	
E		FLOOR 7	KNOWLEDGE	
L		FLOOR 6	PURPOSE	
A		FLOOR 5	PURPOSE	
T		FLOOR 4	PURPOSE	
I		FLOOR 3	PURPOSE	
O		FLOOR 2	PURPOSE	
N		FLOOR 1	PURPOSE	
		FOUNDATION	IDENTITY	

From the beginning of the Bible to the end, from cover to cover, it's full of the revelation of God. In the Old Testament, the revelation of God usually came by the word of a prophet. Once Jesus ascended, He left us with the Holy Spirit to reside and live in us. Now, once we're filled with the Holy Spirit, we have access to revelation anytime we ask and are willing to listen.

Honestly, it's a major advantage over others who don't have the Holy Spirit guiding them. The great thing is, anyone who is in Christ has this revelation available to them. I used the phrase earlier – be willing. I know some major denominations aren't willing to recognize the Holy Spirit as an active force in our lives. They believe He was taken away from us when the disciples died. It makes me sad for people like this. I think this is one of the problems with some churches today.

There is a big difference between the Holy Spirit in your church versus moving in your church. It's like having a power outlet in the wall but never using it for power. It's possible to live in a house full of electricity and power, never plugging into any of the outlets. Things that require power must be plugged in, or they're useless. We are one of the things that requires power. Be sure to plug into the power source (Holy Spirit) and watch how

He moves in and through you.

If you don't believe in the gifts of the Holy Spirit and revelation from God, at the end of this chapter, I'm going to have you participate in an exercise that I'm sure will change your whole thought process about this subject. It's like going through life like a declawed lion with no teeth. You might have the look, but no power to defend yourself. Without the Holy Spirit and His revelation, you will not be able to consume God's Word the way He intends you to because you have no teeth. If you have no teeth, you don't have the ability to take it in as nourishment. As a matter of fact, as I'm writing this book, I just heard the Lord say, *Without the Holy Spirit, you will try to take a bite out of my Word, and because you have no teeth, you will choke on it.* There are parts of the Bible you won't be able to take in and accept because you don't have the Holy Spirit to translate it for you. Think back to the way Jesus talked to His disciples in parables. They couldn't understand many of the things He was saying until He explained it to them. The Holy Spirit does that for us now. I believe we underestimate the word **revelation**. This word must be pretty important to God because He made it the name of the last book of the Bible.

A critical point to remember though is all revelation comes from the Holy Spirit, but the application of His revelation in our lives is up to us.

Prayer: *Father, in the name of Jesus, reveal your Holy Spirit to me. Let Him into my life so that Your free gift of revelation can flow through me. Holy Spirit, I welcome You into my life and allow You to take the lead. Reveal the unknown to me and guide me in a way that I may bring glory and honor to Your name. Help me be a person of influence and direction because Your Holy Spirit and revelation are in me.*

PERSONAL EXAMPLE STATEMENT FOR REVELATION:

I seek the Holy Spirit and pursue His Presence and revelation. I will call on Him in times of need and soak in all He has for me. I will take the time that is needed to be still and silent, waiting on Him.

I've given you an example of what I've done to allow and gain more revelation in my life. Below, I have two questions and one exercise. It's important when you do the exercise, to be in a quiet place, with little to no distractions. I believe this could be the most important part of this entire book.

MY PERSONAL STATEMENT FOR REVELATION:

_____

_____

_____

_____

_____

_____

_____

QUESTIONS:

➢ What have my personal beliefs been on the Holy Spirit and His revelation?

_____

_____

_____

_____

_____

_____

_____

Exercise: *Go to a quiet place with no distractions and simply say this out loud. Take as much time as you need to do this. Be patient and do not rush through. Wait for God to speak to you. I have <u>NO doubt</u> God will show up and speak to you.*

"Holy Spirit, reveal all of Yourself to me and fill me with Your revelation about me and for me."

➢ What did the Holy Spirit say to you during your time of seeking Him out?

_____

_____

_____

_____

_____

_____

_____

CHAPTER 8

READY, SET, GO!

GETTING ACTIVATED
(CHARGED, COMMISSIONED, SENT OUT)

DEFINITION OF ACTIVATION

- : to make active or more active
- : to make (something, such as a molecule) reactive or more reactive
- : to treat so as to improve adsorptive properties
- : to set up or formally institute (an organized group, such as a military unit) with the necessary personnel and equipment
- : to put (an individual or unit) on active duty

The definition of activation is so powerful with phrases like "to become reactive," "improve adsorptive properties," "formally institute," "to put on active duty." I am a Watchman by nature, and God designed me to be activated most of the time, so phrases like in the definition above get my blood flowing! I get very charged being called (activated) to do the work of the Father, actively progressing and advancing the Kingdom of God.

Activation doesn't necessarily mean a literal action. You can be activated and still not move or move in the right direction. Here are some examples of what I'm talking about:

> **Going in the wrong direction.**
>> □ I was watching a football game, and the running back had the ball handed to him (activated), and he became disoriented. He ran into the wrong end zone, ultimately scoring for the wrong team.
>>> • How many times in life have we been given the ball and because of a hard hit or being disoriented, gone the wrong direction and scored a point for the wrong team?
>> □ What about a young person who graduates college with a specific degree (activated), getting confused in

life and ending up back at home, not knowing what direction they want or need to go.

- Just because someone has a degree doesn't mean they know how to move forward with that once they graduate.

☐ What about getting in a car and driving (activated) and accidentally taking a wrong turn and getting lost?

- We've all done this many times. I've even taken a wrong turn while following a GPS!

➢ **Something in the way.**

☐ I can get into my truck in the garage, turn it on, but not be able to move until I open the garage door.

- How many times have we not been able to move because we felt like the door was never opened, or it was closed on us? On a side note, there are urgent times when it's necessary to bust through that door. If I'm in my truck and the garage door is closed, I will get out if necessary and manually open it. If the house is about to explode on the other hand, then I'm throwing it into gear and busting through that door. I get frustrated with some of the "Christianese" phrases that we've all heard:

- *If God closes a door, He will open another one.*
  - What if He wants you to go back to that door and reopen it to test your tenacity?
  - What if He closed that door and locked you in there to protect you from going through the door because what He has for you isn't ready yet?
  - What if He closes the door and puts you in time out? I know He has done this to me many times!
  - Sometimes, He does close the door to open another one. Just be sure you ask why the door was closed. This would be a great time to ask for revelation!
- I've been four-wheeling in the mountains of Colorado many times. There were a few times the roads became impassable due to a landslide, a river too big and deep to cross, a washed-out road, or a large snow drift.
  - Sometimes, we run into impassable circumstances in life. In some of these moments, we just need to turn around and find a different route. Often, it's on that different route that we find what we're looking for.
- ➤ **Never got it in gear.**
  - Anyone who knows even a little about transmissions

knows you can put the vehicle in gear, but if the gears are stripped, you aren't going anywhere.

- How many times has life hit you so hard that your gears felt like they got stripped? I know this has happened to me a few times! These times required a trip to the shop for an overhaul. It's usually as simple as getting into the Word of God and His presence that gives you the spiritual rebuild you need.

➢ **Got stuck.**

☐ I'd like to say that this hasn't happened to me, but that would be a massive lie. I have a very large, beefed up four-door, long bed, diesel Ford truck and I've been stuck in sand, mud, snow, high centered in the middle of a river during a lightning storm, and many other circumstances. One instance I remember being greatly humbled is when my wife had to pull me out of the mud with her "mom" SUV. To my defense, my four-wheel drive was broken.

- Life can get messy, muddy, cold, and wet. Sometimes, we need to have someone there to help us get out of what we're stuck in.

As you can see from the examples above, we can be activated and still not move. Jesus activated us in a major way! He said, *Go into all the nations and share the Gospel.* I consider this a major activation, but why do so many Christians not live out, preach, or share the Gospel? When we receive a revelation from God, that should cause a drive in us that is so strong we cannot be stopped. This is why activation is the next floor above revelation.

STRUCTURE	FLOORS
FLOOR 10	ACTIVATION
FLOOR 9 OPEN ATRIUM	REVELATION
FLOOR 8	WISDOM
FLOOR 7	KNOWLEDGE
FLOOR 6	PURPOSE
FLOOR 5	PURPOSE
FLOOR 4	PURPOSE
FLOOR 3	PURPOSE
FLOOR 2	PURPOSE
FLOOR 1	PURPOSE
FOUNDATION	IDENTITY

R E V E L A T I O N ←

To be activated and move forward, we need to have traction! Traction comes from our identity, purpose, knowledge, wisdom, and revelation. When we follow the progression of building something along these specific steps, we become stronger, more confident, motivated, driven, and can now take ownership of this building called *Striving for the Bottom*.

Once we take ownership and become responsible for something, we need to be a good steward of what God has entrusted us with. We're going to build the next floor of our building called stewardship.

Prayer: *Jesus, please reveal the areas where I've been activated and haven't been able to move or have been going in the wrong direction. Holy Spirit, reveal to me the right doors to go through and which direction to go. Give me traction with knowledge, wisdom, revelation, and the right people who can help pull me out if I get stuck.*

PERSONAL EXAMPLE STATEMENT FOR ACTIVATION:

I will continue to listen to the Holy Spirit and the guidance He is giving me. I will surround myself with people of value who can keep me accountable when I slip up, lose traction, or get stuck in life.

MY PERSONAL STATEMENT FOR ACTIVATION:

_____

_____

_____

_____

_____

_____

_____

QUESTIONS:

➢ Do I feel I am going in the right direction? If so, where am I heading?

_____

_____

_____

_____

_____

_____

_____

➢ If not, what do I need to do to get turned around and going in the right direction?

_____

_____

_____

_____

_____

_____

➢ What might be in the way of where I need to go?

_____

_____

_____

_____

_____

➢ What do I need to do to get myself in gear and moving?

_____

_____

_____

_____

_____

➤ Where am I stuck in life and what do I need to do to get unstuck?

_____

_____

_____

_____

_____

_____

_____

CHAPTER 9

What is Mine, is His
Stewardship

DEFINITION OF STEWARDSHIP

: the office, duties, and obligations of a steward

: the conducting, supervising, or managing of something; *especially*: the careful and responsible management of something entrusted to one's care

Hopefully, we are now getting a sense of the process of *Striving for the Bottom*. We should now have a sense of our identity and our purpose. Just by reading this book, you are pursuing knowledge. Hopefully, you've been talking with others about this book and journey, therefore pursuing wisdom. Then, we asked the Holy Spirit for revelation, and we should now have a clear understanding from Jesus' statement of going into the nations and preaching the Gospel. What does that look like?

I've heard comments such as, *I want to be in ministry*, or *I want to share the Word and be a light for others*. Well, guess what? The moment you became a Christian, you were launched and activated into the ministry. You can be in business, be a pastor, a janitor, a painter, a CEO, a stay-at-home mom, a customer service executive and still be in full-time ministry.

Having stewardship means you have taken responsibility and ownership of what God has given and entrusted you with. One of the greatest ministries you can be a part of is mothering and fathering the younger generations. Notice I said mothering and fathering; I said nothing about actually having your own children.

I am a father to many young people who don't share mine or my wife's DNA. We are all God's children though and all have His DNA, so we're all family. In my opinion, nothing is more important than being a good steward of the younger generations. Stewardship is taking ownership of the next generation, pouring into, loving, and fathering or mothering them. There are so many people who have children but do not father or mother them. I believe one of the greatest issues in the world today is the lack of a father.

Once we feel we've been activated in any calling of our life, we need to be a good steward of it. Therefore, stewardship is the floor above activation.

R		STRUCTURE	FLOORS	
		FLOOR 11	STEWARDSHIP	
E		FLOOR 10	ACTIVATION	
V		FLOOR 9 OPEN ATRIUM	REVELATION	
E				
		FLOOR 8	WISDOM	
L		FLOOR 7	KNOWLEDGE	
A		FLOOR 6	PURPOSE	
		FLOOR 5	PURPOSE	
T		FLOOR 4	PURPOSE	
I		FLOOR 3	PURPOSE	
O		FLOOR 2	PURPOSE	
		FLOOR 1	PURPOSE	
N		FOUNDATION	IDENTITY	

One of the awesome attributes of great stewardship is **increase**. What you take care of and steward well, you will be given more of because you've been faithful with what God has entrusted to you. Think about the parable of the talents:

MATTHEW 25:14-30

[14] "Again, it will be like a man going on a journey, who called his servants and entrusted his wealth to them. [15] To one he gave five bags of gold, to another two bags, and to another one bag, each according to his ability. Then he went on his journey. [16] The man who had received five bags of gold went at once and put his money to work and gained five bags more. [17] So also, the one with two bags of gold gained two more. [18] But the man who had received one bag went off, dug a hole in the ground and hid his master's money. [19] "After a long time the master of those servants returned and settled accounts with them. [20] The man who had received five bags of gold brought the other five. 'Master,' he said, 'you entrusted me with five bags of gold. See, I have gained five more.' [21] "His master replied, 'Well done, good and faithful servant! You have been faithful with a few things; I will put you in charge of

many things. Come and share your master's happiness!' ²² "The man with two bags of gold also came. 'Master,' he said, 'you entrusted me with two bags of gold; see, I have gained two more.' ²³ "His master replied, 'Well done, good and faithful servant! You have been faithful with a few things; I will put you in charge of many things. Come and share your master's happiness!' ²⁴ "Then the man who had received one bag of gold came. 'Master,' he said, 'I knew that you are a hard man, harvesting where you have not sown and gathering where you have not scattered seed. ²⁵ So I was afraid and went out and hid your gold in the ground. See, here is what belongs to you.' ²⁶ "His master replied, 'You wicked, lazy servant! So, you knew that I harvest where I have not sown and gather where I have not scattered seed? ²⁷ Well then, you should have put my money on deposit with the bankers, so that when I returned I would have received it back with interest. ²⁸ "'So take the bag of gold from him and give it to the one who has ten bags. ²⁹ For whoever has will be given more, and they will have an abundance. Whoever does not have, even what they have will be taken from them. ³⁰ And throw that worthless servant outside, into the darkness, where there will be weeping and gnashing of teeth.'

Or the parable of the minas:

LUKE 19:11-27

[11] While they were listening to this, he went on to tell them a parable, because he was near Jerusalem and the people thought that the Kingdom of God was going to appear at once. [12] He said: "A man of noble birth went to a distant country to have himself appointed king and then to return. [13] So he called ten of his servants and gave them ten minas. 'Put this money to work,' he said, 'until I come back.'

[14] "But his subjects hated him and sent a delegation after him to say, 'We don't want this man to be our king.' [15] "He was made king, however, and returned home. Then he sent for the servants to whom he had given the money, in order to find out what they had gained with it. [16] "The first one came and said, 'Sir, your mina has earned ten more.' [17] "'Well done, my good servant!' his master replied. 'Because you have been trustworthy in a very small

matter, take charge of ten cities.'[18] "The second came and said, 'Sir, your mina has earned five more.' [19] "His master answered, 'You take charge of five cities.'[20] "Then another servant came and said, 'Sir, here is your mina; I have kept it laid away in a piece of cloth. [21] I was afraid of you, because you are a hard man. You take out what you did not put in and reap what you did not sow.'[22] "His master replied, 'I will judge you by your own words, you wicked servant! You knew, did you, that I am a hard man, taking out what I did not put in, and reaping what I did not sow? [23] Why then didn't you put my money on deposit, so that when I came back, I could have collected it with interest?'[24] "Then he said to those standing by, 'Take his mina away from him and give it to the one who has ten minas.'[25] "'Sir,' they said, 'he already has ten!' [26] "He replied, 'I tell you that to everyone who has, more will be given, but as for the one who has nothing, even what they have will be taken away. [27] But those enemies of mine who did not want me to be king over them—bring them here and kill them in front of me.'"

These two parables scare the snot out of me and encourage me at the same time. God does not take it lightly when you have poor stewardship of what He has given you! But look at what God did when they were good stewards and faithful with what they were given! This is so exciting! What they were given was doubled.

Now let's say they continued to be good stewards and faithful with what God gave them, the doubling would never stop. I think people accidentally look past this. Ten becomes 20, and 20 becomes 40, and 40 becomes 80, and 80 becomes 160, and 160 becomes 320, and 320 becomes 640, and 640 becomes 1280, and 1280 becomes 2560, and 2560 becomes 5120, and 5120 becomes 10,240. I think you get my point. God is the God of multiplication, not addition. You might even say that when you aren't a good steward, you not only miss out on the doubling...you also miss out on the opportunity for future blessings **and** multiplication!

It's also important to recognize that this is not about money. In the parable of the minas, because they were good stewards of the minas, they were given cities. Let's be sure to not overlook the consequences of bad stewardship. The man who did nothing:

³⁰ And throw that worthless servant outside, into the darkness, where there will be weeping and gnashing of teeth.'

I don't want to be that guy! I want to be the one receiving more! Good stewardship and receiving rewards cause you to have confidence in what you are doing. Building confidence leads to boldness which is the next floor in our building called *Striving for the Bottom.*

Prayer: *Jesus, thank You for trusting me with all You have given me. Thank You for allowing me to prove myself in all that I do. Please help me be worthy of my calling by giving me the ability to expand my territories of influence through knowledge, wisdom, and revelation of Your Holy Spirit.*

PERSONAL EXAMPLE COMMITMENT TO STEWARDSHIP:

I will hold dear to me all that You have given me. I will be a good steward of my purpose, wife, children, family, friends, calling, and possessions. I will do my best through the Holy Spirit to multiply all that I've been entrusted with.

I've given you an example of what I've done to be a good steward of what God has called me to and entrusted me with.

Now, what have you done and what will you do to be a good steward of what God has given you?

MY PERSONAL COMMITMENT TO STEWARDSHIP:

_____

_____

_____

_____

_____

_____

QUESTIONS:

➢ How have I done in the areas of stewardship in my life?

_____

_____

_____

_____

_____

➤ Where have I done well?

_____

_____

_____

_____

_____

_____

➤ Where can I improve?

_____

_____

_____

_____

_____

_____

CHAPTER 10

NO FEAR
WALKING IN BOLDNESS

DEFINITION OF BOLD

: fearless before danger

: showing or requiring a fearless daring spirit: a *bold* plan

: standing out prominently: *bold* headlines

B oldness can be conveyed as passion. You can always tell when someone walks in boldness because they cannot be intimidated or stopped in fulfilling their purpose. They usually live a fearless life. Boldness is the next floor in our building called *Striving for the Bottom*. I know it may seem weird to strive for the bottom with boldness and passion, but I assure you that you'll soon find out why we need to pursue the bottom with all our heart and being!

I know I've been repetitive throughout this book, but it's very intentional. Often, it takes hearing a truth many times before it truly sinks in and saturates our whole being. Boldness is a response to receiving and fulfilling the purpose that God has laid out before us.

How can we just sit around in a world that is hurting and lost and not do anything? The next time you're in a store, mall, restaurant, gas station, or church, take some time and look into people's eyes. If we take the time to look into people's eyes, we can easily see lost, hurting, confused, and bitter people. Then we need to ask the Holy Spirit to reveal what it is that's troubling them, and from His revelation, we can then minister to them with the Love of Jesus.

These actions of compassion, concern, and just wanting to help them demonstrate being a good steward of what God has called us to do. Just asking someone, *what's the matter?* or *how can I pray for you?* is boldness in action. Being a good steward of what He has given us will automatically create a drive to be bold in our actions and not allow anything to come between us and our God-given purpose. As you can see in the next figure, our building is getting pretty tall and big.

	STRUCTURE	FLOORS
R	FLOOR 12	BOLDNESS
E	FLOOR 11	STEWARDSHIP
V	FLOOR 10	ACTIVATION
E	FLOOR 9 OPEN ATRIUM	REVELATION
L	FLOOR 8	WISDOM
	FLOOR 7	KNOWLEDGE
A	FLOOR 6	PURPOSE
T	FLOOR 5	PURPOSE
	FLOOR 4	PURPOSE
I	FLOOR 3	PURPOSE
O	FLOOR 2	PURPOSE
	FLOOR 1	PURPOSE
N	FOUNDATION	IDENTITY

The awesome benefit of having a big, tall building is that a lot of people can live in it. The building should be a metaphor for our lives. When we have the love of God, there are no limits on who we can share it with. Our home is rather large with a big backyard, a big pool, and a huge fire pit. When my wife and I bought this property, we knew the purpose of it was to be a place for gathering people, laughing, ministering, having fun, watching children running around and play, and most importantly, be a home of peace and rest. I love knowing that whoever visits our home will be loved and protected.

Boldness is mentioned all throughout the Bible: David facing the giant, Daniel standing up for his beliefs, Paul sharing the Gospel relentlessly, Elijah confronting the prophets of Baal, and Gideon taking a massive city with 300 men. I could go on and on. Boldness empowers us to be fearless in our actions and leads us to live supernatural lifestyles. Scripture also talks about another type of boldness:

HEBREWS 4:16

So let us come boldly to the throne of our gracious God. There we will receive his mercy, and we will find grace to help us when we need it most.

This type of boldness brings me comfort knowing that my Father is approachable at any time. I don't have to be afraid of Him. He is merciful, and when I mess up, which we all do, I can come to Him with a repentant heart, and He will give me love and grace because He's a loving Father. I know this can be hard for some of us to wrap our brains around because we may have had a challenging childhood, but this Father is perfect in every way. As a father of four, I can see this through my children. When they mess up, there will be consequences, but it will never change my love for them. Nothing will ever change how much I love them.

Knowing you are loved unconditionally can also produce boldness because you will be willing to take more risks and challenges without the fear of wrath from our Father. Now I do need to balance this out a little. We are not selfish, deceitful, or manipulative in our intent. Intentional sin is different than unintentional sin. The easy way to distinguish between the two is to look at the posture of our heart at the time of the sin. The consequence of my children intentionally messing up will be greater versus accidentally messing up.

Boldness, confidence, self-assurance, courage, bravery, audacity, and valor are all close friends. If anyone associates me with the words above, I'd be totally fine with that. Regardless of being a man or woman, young or old, rich or poor, we're all called to be bold, confident, brave, and fearless for the Lord.

I often wonder why we sabotage ourselves at times. Why do some Christians purposefully allow fearful things into their lives? Worthless stuff such as horror movies, haunted houses, grotesque video games, etc. When the Bible says, "perfect love casts out fear," it doesn't make sense to bring fear into our life through our actions. The Bible also says a kingdom divided against itself cannot stand. Often, we wonder why we do not or cannot walk in a place of boldness and fearlessness. It's because only in *perfect love* can we be truly bold and fearless.

Boldness is often associated with being selfless. Think about a soldier charging into battle with boldness, not thinking about themselves, but the mission they have been charged with. Boldness in the Kingdom is what makes us unstoppable, willing to take on anything the Lord has placed in front of us regardless of the challenges or obstacles we may face. Boldness without accomplishment though is empty and useless. A lion in a cage roaring boldly at the top of his lungs is no threat to me. A lion in a cage cannot fulfill its calling as king of the Serengeti while it's in a cage. Boldness is only effective in the environment we were designed to be in, the front lines, advancing the Kingdom. The result of boldness is fruition. Fruition is the next floor in the building, *Striving for the Bottom*.

Prayer: *Holy Spirit, give me the heart of a lion, being fearless in all that You call me to do and be. Help me recognize places I have allowed fear into my life and to be diligent in casting fear out of my life so that I may love like You love.*

PERSONAL EXAMPLE COMMITMENT TO BOLDNESS:

I will be bold and fearless in all that God has called me to do. I will do my best to love with the love of God so that I will not be afraid in my life because perfect Love casts out all fear. I will guard my eyes, ears, and heart against things that represent fear. I will approach Your throne with boldness as You said I could do and be what You called me to be without question.

I have given you an example of what I have done to be bold and what I will do to continue to live as a bold warrior for the Kingdom. How will you live a life with boldness?

MY PERSONAL COMMITMENT TO BOLDNESS:

_____

_____

_____

_____

_____

_____

_____

QUESTIONS:

➤ Which areas of my life do I allow fear to enter?

_____

_____

_____

_____

_____

_____

➤ What will I do to remove the fear, so I can walk in boldness?

_____

_____

_____

_____

_____

_____

CHAPTER 11

BEING FRUITY
EXPERIENCING FRUITION

DEFINITION OF FRUITION

- : pleasurable use or possession
- : the state of bearing fruit
- : the point at which a plan or project is realized
- : an occasion when a plan or an idea begins to happen, exist, or be successful
- : the state of having successfully completed an activity or plan

Once we have reached this floor, we can start to see actual, tangible results and their effects on others. Fruition in our lives produces nutrition for others. It's when we strive for something—a goal, dream, or plan—that we start to see it come to life.

Think of it like this. We plant a peach tree (identity), which is to produce food (purpose). We learn how to grow a peach tree (knowledge) and take extra care in raising it in the right environment (wisdom). I get this feeling there's about to be a massive hailstorm coming, so I cover it with a large tarp barrier (revelation). My boss informed me that this is a special tree and to take great care of it (activation). So I go out every day and make sure there aren't any bugs or squirrels trying to eat the fruit as it starts to produce (stewardship). One day I see a wild hog starting to dig out the tree to eat it, and I run out with a stick and chase off the hog (boldness). After many months of taking care of this tree, big, juicy peaches are ripe. I grab one and bite into it! The peach is bursting with juices and a super sweet flavor (fruition).

I don't know about you, but my mouth is watering right now. I have a peach tree in my yard, so I'm going to go eat a ripe, juicy peach!

Funny thing, we can spend all of our time caring for something and toward the end, lose everything because of a lack of follow through, laziness, or taking it for granted. I haven't looked at the peach tree for a few days. I looked closely, and about half of the peaches were damaged because birds had been eating them. When it takes so much time and energy to produce the perfect peach, to give up on it at the end is such a waste of your time. I've watched people build businesses, make sacrifices, stretch every penny, work long hours, and become very successful, only to lose everything because they made poor choices or took some other careless action.

Fruition can be heartbreaking and devastating if we don't actually get to enjoy the harvest we've worked so hard for. I recall watching a documentary on farmers in America. They followed these farmers throughout the farming process— from the preparation of the field, planting of the seed, caring for the wheat, to the time of harvest. Most of the farmers had a great harvest, but a few did not. Right before the harvest, a tornado and hailstorm swept through the region and destroyed everything! You could see the defeated look in their eyes. A reporter asked them, *what are you going to do now?* Without hesitation one farmer replied, *we will plant again when it is time.* After everything he'd been through, he responded with boldness in his heart. As I said before, when you know who you are, why you're here, attain knowledge, seek wisdom and revelation, act upon your task, are a good steward of what you have been given, carry boldness, and are not moved by circumstances, fruition *will* happen.

	STRUCTURE	FLOORS	
R	FLOOR 13	FRUITION	
	FLOOR 12	BOLDNESS	
E	FLOOR 11	STEWARDSHIP	
V	FLOOR 10	ACTIVATION	
E	FLOOR 9 OPEN ATRIUM	REVELATION	←
L	FLOOR 8	WISDOM	
	FLOOR 7	KNOWLEDGE	
A	FLOOR 6	PURPOSE	
T	FLOOR 5	PURPOSE	
	FLOOR 4	PURPOSE	
I	FLOOR 3	PURPOSE	
O	FLOOR 2	PURPOSE	
	FLOOR 1	PURPOSE	
N	FOUNDATION	IDENTITY	

STRIVING FOR THE BOTTOM

What does God think when someone reaches this level and does not produce fruit? Well, there just happens to be Scripture for that.

MATTHEW 3:10

"The axe is already laid at the root of the trees; therefore, every tree that does not bear good fruit is cut down and thrown into the fire.

As a Christian, you can see from Matthew 3:10 what God thinks about us not producing fruit. I see a lot of people who call themselves Christians, but don't produce the fruit of a Christian. What are the fruits of a non-Christian and a Christian?

NON-CHRISTIAN: GALATIANS 5:19-21

[19] The acts of the flesh are obvious: sexual immorality, impurity, and debauchery; [20] idolatry and witchcraft; hatred, discord, jealousy, fits of rage, selfish ambition, dissensions, factions [21] and envy; drunkenness, orgies, and the like. I warn you, as I did before, that those who live like this will not inherit the Kingdom of God.

CHRISTIAN: GALATIANS 5:22-23

²² But the fruit of the Spirit is love, joy, peace, forbearance, kindness, goodness, faithfulness, ²³ gentleness, and self-control. Against such things, there is no law.

We are known by the fruit we produce, plain and simple! That being said, no one is perfect, and we all make mistakes, but mistakes are temporal and Godly fruition is eternal. What type of life do you choose to live?

MATTHEW 12:33-37

³³ "Either make the tree good and its fruit good or make the tree bad and its fruit bad; for the tree is known by its fruit. ³⁴ "You brood of vipers, how can you, being evil, speak what is good? For the mouth speaks out of that which fills the heart. ³⁵ "The good man brings out of his good treasure what is good, and the evil man brings out of his evil treasure what is evil. ³⁶ "But I tell you that every careless word that people speak, they shall give an accounting for it in the day of judgment. ³⁷ "For by your words you will be justified, and by your words, you will be condemned."

If we plan on making it to Heaven, we need to produce good, healthy, sweet, nutritious, Godly fruit. Why is fruit used in the Bible as an example of fulfillment? Well, I believe the attributes of fruit can apply to all the areas of our lives. Fruit nourishes and produces from itself. Every piece of fruit has a seed, able to produce more of itself for countless generations to come. I can hold a single peach in my hand, but only God knows how many peaches will come from it. When we experience fruition, we can reach the top floor of mentorship. In the next chapter, I will go over mentorship. It has become one of my greatest passions and loves in life!

Prayer: *Father, thank You for allowing me to come to fruition and provide resources and advancement for You. Please protect me from the attacks of the enemy and allow the fruit in me to grow to its full potential and be harvested for others to enjoy. Bless all that I do and set my hands in action for You.*

PERSONAL EXAMPLE COMMITMENT TO FRUITION:

I will protect the soil and environment in my life, so the right elements are created, and I become the most productive I can be. I will seek out knowledge, wisdom, and revelation so I can know how to be a good steward of what You have entrusted me with.

I've given you an example of what fruition looks like for me and how I will continue to produce all the fruit I am designed to produce. What is your commitment?

MY PERSONAL COMMITMENT TO FRUITION:

_____

_____

_____

_____

_____

_____

_____

QUESTIONS:

➢ In which areas of my life do I produce good fruit?

_____

_____

_____

_____

_____

_____

➢ In which areas of my life do I produce bad fruit?

_____

_____

_____

_____

_____

➢ What will I do to increase fruition in my life?

_____

_____

_____

_____

_____

_____

➢ What will I do to protect the fruition in my life?

_____

_____

_____

_____

_____

_____

CHAPTER 12

THE MOST REWARDING CALL

ACHIEVING MENTORSHIP

(FATHERING / MOTHERING)

DEFINITION OF MENTOR

: a trusted counselor, teacher or guide

: an influential senior sponsor or supporter

Mentoring is one of my favorite things to do in life—whether it's one-on-one or a huge group of people. Helping someone walk through life is one of the greatest honors I have. I love taking time with people to share mistakes

I've made in life and how I overcame them. I often share the battles I've been through and the wounds that have scarred which now serve as reminders of the battles I've fought.

It's important to follow and be mentored by someone who has scars, a limp, healed wounds, and not follow someone who walks with a strut and has no battle wounds. It's in the battles of life that we are tested, strengthened, and proven. These ideal warriors we'll follow have fought the good fight and can encourage us when we go through our own battles. We live in a world where the strong, determined, and identity-driven will thrive. The one I follow most has scars on His hands, feet, side, and back. I choose to be led by those who are willing to go into battle ready to conquer all of the trials that they'll come across.

We need to be bold and willing to share where we've messed up so the ones we mentor can avoid the same mistakes. By avoiding the same mistakes, they can go farther than ourselves because we cared about them enough to highlight the hazards of life and how to avoid them. I think a major problem with the church today is the line that the congregation and leadership draw between the pulpit and the congregation.

Some leaders portray a position of power that makes the congregation believe it's impossible for them to be as Godly, move in power effectively, change the world, or share the love of Jesus because they're not part of leadership. I think the congregation becomes "pew sitters" and uses the excuse that sharing and living the life of Jesus is the responsibility of the leadership. The reality is that we all lead and influence people every day of our lives and will all be accountable before God on how we lived and accepted the purpose and calling He gave us. We need to erase the line between the pulpit and the congregation and work together to advance the Kingdom, ultimately leading to more saved souls.

As mentors, we need to empower anyone and everyone to know they can make a difference. We can achieve all things through Christ who strengthens us. There is no one more important than another in the Body of Christ. Everyone has their own calling and purpose in life, and we are designed by God to be the best at what we are called to be. When we experience fruition in our lives, we can then mentor others. It is our God-given responsibility. Mentorship is the top floor in the building of life! It's at this level that we can embrace what *Striving for the Bottom* means.

STRUCTURE	FLOORS
FLOOR 14	MENTORSHIP
FLOOR 13	FRUITION
FLOOR 12	BOLDNESS
FLOOR 11	STEWARDSHIP
FLOOR 10	ACTIVATION
FLOOR 9 OPEN ATRIUM	REVELATION
FLOOR 8	WISDOM
FLOOR 7	KNOWLEDGE
FLOOR 6	PURPOSE
FLOOR 5	PURPOSE
FLOOR 4	PURPOSE
FLOOR 3	PURPOSE
FLOOR 2	PURPOSE
FLOOR 1	PURPOSE
FOUNDATION	IDENTITY

R E V E L A T I O N

Mentorship is a massive responsibility. We are responsible and accountable for our actions in the life that we live. I've established an order of importance for my mentorship.

As a mentor, the greatest reflection of my success is:

1) **My relationship with Jesus;**

2) **My relationship with my wife;**

3) **My relationship with my children;**
4) **My relationship with my friends; and last**
5) **The success of my business.**

**A public success and a private failure is
an overall 100% failure!**

If you don't have your life in the right order, how can you mentor others? If we don't know our **identity** or **purpose**, how can we mentor others? If we haven't sought out **knowledge**, **wisdom**, and **revelation**, how can we mentor others? If we haven't **activated** ourselves, exemplifying good **stewardship**, walking in **boldness** and living a life of **fruition**, how can we mentor others? Living all these things out is why this building needs to be built in the order it is. God designed us to live life to its fullest, loving people with His Love, and pouring (mentoring) into others!

As I said before, this is not a male or female, black, white, yellow, brown, or pink with purple polka dots thing. If we live how God has intended us to live, we can all mentor people. I've helped thousands of older people over the years, and I've come to a conclusion—I believe you can usually tell if a person lived a self-centered life only thinking about themselves. These are the ones who spend their later years lonely, angry, and bitter. They end up dying alone, wondering why no one wants to be around them.

The opposite seems to be true as well. You can tell who's spent their life pouring into, mentoring, and loving others. In their later years, they're surrounded by people who want to be around them because they are still pouring into, mentoring, and loving people. If you are truly a mentor, there will never be a need for retirement because you will never want to. An awesome thing about this later stage of life is, you will witness the multiple generations of people that you mentor grow up and live their lives how God designed them to. Talk about a rewarding way to live the last part of our lives.

There is never a stage of life when it's too late to start mentoring. I still see this now. You have two types of people in their later years:

- **Person 1** – I'm too old, too lazy, too tired, too self-centered, too full of self-pity, too selfish, too this, too that, to take the time to mentor others.
- **Person 2** – I'm full of the Spirit of God and cannot contain myself. I'm overflowing with His love and cannot help but share the Love of God, and the grace

He has poured out over my life. I will live until my last breath, pouring my life out to others!

Which person do you want to be? Which life do you want to live? Some of the greatest lessons in life I've ever learned have been from my elders. Some of the most impactful moments I've experienced have been expressed by people in their final dying moments.

Think about how Jesus mentored us in His final days:

IN THE GARDEN:

Luke 22:42 "Father, if you are willing, take this cup from me; yet not my will, but yours be done."

ON THE CROSS:

Luke 23:34 Jesus said, "Father, forgive them, for they do not know what they are doing." And they divided up his clothes by casting lots.

Luke 23:39-43 [39] One of the criminals who hung there hurled insults at him: "Aren't you the Messiah? Save yourself and us!" [40] But the other criminal rebuked him. "Don't you fear God," he said, "since you are under the same sentence? [41] We are punished justly, for we are getting what our deeds deserve. But this man has done nothing wrong." [42] Then he said, "Jesus, remember me when you come into your Kingdom." [43] Jesus answered him, "Truly I tell you, today you will be with me in paradise."

John 19:25-27 [25] Near the cross of Jesus stood his mother, his mother's sister, Mary the wife of Clopas, and Mary Magdalene. [26] When Jesus saw his mother there, and the disciple whom he loved standing nearby, he said to her, "Woman, here is your son," [27] and to the disciple, "Here is your mother." From that time on, this disciple took her into his home.

Matthew 27:45-46 [45] From noon until three in the afternoon darkness came over all the land. [46] About three in the afternoon Jesus cried out in a loud voice, "Eli, Eli, lema sabachthani?" (which means "My God, my God, why have you forsaken me?").

Luke 23:46 Jesus called out with a loud voice, "Father, into your hands I commit my spirit." When he had said this, he breathed his last.

You can see from the Scriptures that Jesus, the Son of God, in the most brutal, horrific moments experienced by a man in history, right before His death, was mentoring us! We are to model our lives after His example. Here is the crazy, blow-your-mind moment: Jesus said we would do greater things than Him!

JOHN 14:12-14

[12] Very truly I tell you, whoever believes in me will do the works I have been doing, and they will do even greater things than these because I am going to the Father. [13] And I will do whatever you ask in my name, so that the Father may be glorified in the Son. [14] You may ask me for anything in my name, and I will do it.

This Scripture still blows my mind! If Jesus, in His last moments, loved us so much that He would mentor us from the cross, then what should we do? We have no excuse but to live for more than ourselves. One of the incredible revelations of this book stems from the title, *Striving for the Bottom*. When we achieve the ability to mentor, we are no longer at the top, but the bottom. We become a servant to the ones we are mentoring, helping and guiding through life.

Prayer: *Jesus, even on the cross, while You were suffering in great anguish, Your thoughts were for us. You are the perfect example of how to live life and therefore provide a perfect model for us to follow. Help us to see others through Your eyes, so that we may see the person for who they are meant to be, not who they are right now. Give us the revelation You have for their lives. All we want is a heart like Yours and to love how You love. Thank You for being a great and perfect mentor.*

PERSONAL EXAMPLE COMMITMENT TO BE A MENTOR:

I will choose to see others through the eyes of Jesus, mentoring and pouring into those set before me. I will give those in front of me grace and mercy during the tough and trying times. I will always continue to grow myself through the reading of God's Word and soaking in His Presence. I will always strive for those I mentor to be greater and go farther than I could without being threatened or envious of their advancement. I will celebrate their accomplishments. I will not hold back anything that needs to be said at the appropriate time. I will live my life as best as I can to be an example of what it looks like to be a son of God, a loving husband, and father. I will be an ethical and moral leader in all my life, living as an ambassador of our Heavenly Father.

I have given you a pretty clear understanding of what mentorship is and why it's so important to live a life of mentoring others. Write your commitment below.

MY PERSONAL COMMITMENT TO BE A MENTOR:

_____

_____

_____

_____

_____

_____

_____

QUESTIONS:

➢ Who is someone I know that I could mentor?

_____

_____

_____

_____

_____

_____

_____

➢ How and when will I reach out to that person?

_____

_____

_____

_____

_____

_____

_____

➢ What will I do to stay committed to never abandoning the person or people I will mentor?

_____

_____

_____

_____

_____

_____

CHAPTER 13

LIVING AT THE BOTTOM
LIVING A LIFE OF SERVANTHOOD

DEFINITION OF SERVANTHOOD

: one that serves others

Great mentors are never afraid of those they mentor surpassing them. Great mentors celebrate those moments. A true mentor never has a problem living at the bottom as a servant to others and wishes nothing but the best for everyone they encounter, always seeing the God-given potential in their lives. Paul talks about this in Philippians 2:1-7 where he shares how Jesus modeled servanthood for us:

PHILIPPIANS 2:1-7

Therefore, if you have any encouragement from being united with Christ, if any comfort from his love, if any common sharing in the Spirit, if any tenderness and compassion, [2] then make my joy complete by being like-minded, having the same love, being one in spirit and of one mind. [3] Do nothing out of selfish ambition or vain conceit. Rather, in humility value others above yourselves, [4] not looking to your own interests but each of you to the interests of the others. [5] In your relationships with one another, have the same mindset as Christ Jesus: [6] Who, being in very nature God, did not consider equality with God something to be used to his own advantage; [7] rather, he made himself nothing by taking the very nature of a servant, being made in human likeness.

I think some of the greatest issues throughout world history are pride and misfocused competition. People and churches have this need to feel like they must compete for recognition from others and are constantly competing with the people around them. That mindset is full of pride and poverty thinking! Why is it poverty thinking?

Poverty thinking makes you believe there is a limited amount of something. We aren't competing for souls from our fellow churches or people we mentor. It sickens me to think that churches and pastors worry that other churches around them are doing better or have a bigger congregation. Just go to the local school, grocery store, mall, gas station, or even your own church to see that there are more than enough people who need Jesus and our mentorship. Competition and pride have no place in the Kingdom when your heart is set on striving for and living at the bottom as a servant. Even Jesus had to address this with His disciples, and we are to model how He handles it.

LUKE 22:24-27

24 Now a dispute also arose among them as to which of them was regarded to be the greatest. 25 Jesus said to them, "The kings of the Gentiles have absolute power *and* lord it over them; and those in authority over them are called 'Benefactors.' 26 But it is not to be this way with you; on the contrary, the one who is the greatest among you must become like the youngest [and least privileged], and the [one who is the] leader, like the servant. 27 For who is the

greater, the one who reclines *at the table* or the one who serves? Is it not the one who reclines *at the table*? But I am among you as the one who serves.

Jesus modeled that the top in the Kingdom is actually living at the bottom. The Bible is full of examples that are contradictory to what the world thinks. The world's idea of success is living at the top, living a life that is superior to others.

Look at some of the ways the Hollywood celebrities, the ultra-wealthy folks, and the famous people portray themselves but are actually a total mess and miserable on the inside. Not all are like that, but it appears that many living at the top, are emotionally, physically, and spiritually in the lowest of the low. There are so many Scriptures that talk about bottom living. I've put a few in this book, but I would highly recommend doing a study on a bottom-living lifestyle.

MARK 9:35

And he sat down and called the twelve. And he said to them, "If anyone would be first, he must be last of all and servant of all."

1 PETER 4:10

As each has received a gift, use it to serve one another, as good stewards of God's varied grace:

JOHN 15:12-13

[12] "This is my commandment, that you love one another as I have loved you. [13] Greater love has no one than this, that someone lay down his life for his friends.

2 CORINTHIANS 4:5

[5] For what we proclaim is not ourselves, but Jesus Christ as Lord, with ourselves as your servants for Jesus' sake.

As you can see, Jesus is consistent in His instruction about living life as a servant. You can see from the final illustration of our *Striving for the Bottom* building, that we are not trying to reach the top floor, but the basement.

STRUCTURE	FLOORS
FLOOR 14	MENTORSHIP
FLOOR 13	FRUITION
FLOOR 12	BOLDNESS
FLOOR 11	STEWARDSHIP
FLOOR 10	ACTIVATION
FLOOR 9 OPEN ATRIUM	REVELATION
FLOOR 8	WISDOM
FLOOR 7	KNOWLEDGE
FLOOR 6	PURPOSE
FLOOR 5	PURPOSE
FLOOR 4	PURPOSE
FLOOR 3	PURPOSE
FLOOR 2	PURPOSE
FLOOR 1	PURPOSE
FOUNDATION	IDENTITY
BASEMENT	SERVANTHOOD

R E V E L A T I O N

When we're in the basement, we get to help and support the people we mentor. Through mentoring, we get to help them discover Identity, Purpose, Knowledge, Wisdom, Revelation, Activation, Stewardship, Boldness, Fruition, and Mentorship. The ultimate goal of servanthood is to model what Jesus did for us, taking us to the highest level we can go, which is Heaven to be with Him.

The older I get, the more I realize how desperately we need to live this lifestyle. Life is about elevating others to see farther than we ever could. If you have children, I'm sure you have modeled this yourself without ever realizing how much you have. Every time you pick up your child, you are elevating him or her. Even when you pick up your baby because they are crying or your little one falls, you pick them up to comfort and calm them. You pick them up to help them move a little faster or protect them while they are in a parking lot with you.

We went to Disneyland when my kids were very young, and I remember my oldest not being able to see something she wanted to see because she was too small. I saw this and could see her frustration, so I picked her up and put her on my shoulders. By doing this, I elevated her higher than myself, and she could see farther than I could. It's the perfect example of how we are to mentor others, by lifting others to see farther than we ever could. At that moment, she had a huge smile on her face, and I was filled with joy because she could see even beyond what she longed to see. I never got jealous, envious, or felt like I got the bad end of the deal. I celebrated with her and in her joy. This is how we need to live; celebrating other people's successes in the Kingdom.

What if you don't have children? Well, you don't need to have children to father or mother someone. I think about the times when I was playing with a friend, and we wanted to climb up to a place we couldn't get to without the assistance of one another. Or someone falls or trips in front of us, and we reach down to pick them up. We may not realize it but lifting others up in times of need is a God-given attribute that He instilled in us. We have been lifting people up throughout our entire lives without even thinking about it.

True mentorship is being a seed that dies to itself, therefore producing and growing in life by serving others.

Prayer: *Jesus, You are the perfect example of being a selfless servant, always with our best interest in Your heart. Fill us up with Your love, that way we do not feel the need to compete with anyone else in the Kingdom. Allow us to see beyond our own pride and self-interest so that we may live and be fulfilled in and through a life of servanthood.*

PERSONAL EXAMPLE COMMITMENT TO A LIFE OF SERVANTHOOD:

I will choose to live a life of servanthood, looking out for the opportunities to serve and lift others up. I will not allow pride or competition with others to get in the way of living at the bottom. I will have joy and celebrate when others surpass me. I will choose to live the example Jesus set for me as the ultimate servant, giving up His life for me.

I have given you a clear understanding and example through Jesus of true and pure servanthood. I've also given you my personal commitment to servanthood. What does a commitment to servanthood look like for you?

MY PERSONAL COMMITMENT TO A LIFE OF SERVANTHOOD:

_____

_____

_____

_____

_____

_____

_____

QUESTIONS:

➢ Who is someone I can serve right now?

_____

_____

_____

_____

_____

_____

➢ What do I do to keep pride and a competitive spirit away when trying to reach the lost?

_____

_____

_____

_____

_____

_____

➢ What will I do to stay committed to serving and lifting others up?

_____

_____

_____

_____

_____

_____

CHAPTER 14

CONCLUSION

When the Lord told me to write this book, He gave me the title, wisdom, and revelation to write the first draft in seven days. It was over 20,000 words. I still had other responsibilities at that time which makes it even more amazing.

The urgency was set so strong in my heart to write this book because the Holy Spirit stressed to me that the longer I wait to listen to Him about writing this book, the longer people will suffer and struggle through life without knowing their real identity and purpose. There are people right now who are called to mentor but haven't yet stepped into their role because no one has spoken into them. I feel like many people have a book in their heart that the Lord has set for them, but they haven't yet pulled the trigger for reasons such as busyness or the inability to express thoughts through writing. These are all excuses that should be overcome. If the Lord has put the idea of writing a book on your heart, don't you believe He'll meet any shortcoming you may think you have? People's futures depend on your willingness and obedience to do what He has called you to do. Step up and step out. Be bold in your activation. Don't let the enemy tell you lies and influence your purposes in life.

I realize now that the whole reason I'm writing this book is that I'm tired of seeing people hurting. I've been alive for over four decades and have done many dumb and careless things that have caused my body an enormous amount of pain. I have broken my sternum twice, torn muscles from my abdominal wall, sprained my back, cracked ribs, and suffered many other injuries. I learned only a few years ago to be more cautious in the way I do things because I'm tired of physical pain and recovery.

The same things apply to actions I have or have not done and things I have or have not said. There are times I should've stopped and loved someone more or listened more instead of talking. There are times I should've had more compassion for a situation. There are times I should've stopped and ministered to someone, and I didn't. I'm tired of experiencing or causing others emotional pain because my mouth or heart got in the way. I will never get those missed opportunities again but going forward, I can make sure I don't miss them the next time they come around.

I pray this book and advice has given you identity from the Father, purpose for your life, and motivation to seek the knowledge necessary to fulfill your purpose. I pray that you will pursue wisdom and activate wisdom with the revelation of the Holy Spirit. That revelation will activate you to become a good steward, walking in boldness, and charging forward without fear or doubt. I pray that your life and all you do would be an example of Kingdom fruition, which allows you to step into mentorship with confidence through Christ. I pray that you would have a servant's heart and that you would live life *Striving for the Bottom!*